Smart Wealth Building

Modern Buy and Hold Real Estate Investing

James A. Long

Table of Contents

Chapter 1: Introduction to Smart Wealth Building

A purposeful and contemporary approach to achieving financial stability and success is represented by smart wealth building. Beyond the conventional ideas of saving and investing, it adopts a dynamic methodology that makes use of modern tools and tactics, with a concentration on real estate in particular.

Table of Contents

At its foundation, smart wealth building challenges people to consider options other than living paycheck to paycheck, including making their money work for them. This strategy entails making well-informed decisions regarding a variety of financial matters, including judicious investing, asset leveraging, and investigating opportunities for passive income generation.

Intelligent real estate investing, particularly using the "buy and hold" strategy, is one of the main foundations of building smart wealth. This tactic involves purchasing properties with the purpose of keeping them for an extended period of time so they can increase in value and produce rental revenue. Real estate has many benefits, including the possibility of tax benefits, asset diversification, and inflation protection, which are all recognized by smart wealth builders.

Essentially, smart wealth building is about approaching personal money with a forward-looking and proactive mindset. It motivates people to seek financial education, support creativity, and make the most of contemporary tools and technologies to make wise judgments. It's a way of thinking that enables individuals to take charge of their financial futures and leave a legacy of financial security for their families and themselves.

1.1: The Development of Real Estate Investing

Over the years, real estate investing has changed dramatically, influenced by shifting societal choices, technological breakthroughs, and shifting economic conditions. Anyone hoping to succeed in the current real estate market must comprehend this evolution.

In the beginning, real estate investing was frequently reserved for the affluent elite who could afford to buy big plots of land or expensive properties. Rent was paid in cash or kind, and the market was rather small-scale. For most people, the idea of universal real estate investment is just a pipe dream.

When the 20th century arrived, real estate investing began to become more widely available. It became simpler for the middle class to acquire homes and investment properties thanks to the widespread availability of mortgage finance. The emergence of real estate investment trusts (REITs) made it possible for even small investors to indirectly participate in the real estate market. The "buy and hold" approach, where investors purchased homes for long-term appreciation and rental income, became more popular during this time.

With the use of technology in real estate, the 21st century brought about a fundamental change. Investors can pool funds and access a variety of assets thanks to online platforms and crowdfunding. Predictive analytics and tools made it possible to make better-informed investing decisions. Real estate has also gained popularity as a potent asset class for portfolio diversification. Today, investors can take advantage of the international character of real estate markets and explore opportunities all over the world without being restricted by geographic boundaries.

Looking ahead, we can see that real estate investing is still evolving. Green and sustainability programs are becoming more popular, and smart home technology is improving tenant and property management. Along with this, the sector is adjusting to shifting demographics and consumer tastes, with an increased emphasis on urbanization trends and flexible living spaces. Investors who want to take advantage of the opportunities and innovations that characterize modern real estate investing must fully comprehend this dynamic market.

1.2: Understanding the Buy-and-Hold Approach

The buy-and-hold technique, which emphasizes a patient, long-term attitude toward property ownership, is the cornerstone of successful real estate investing. This strategy is based on the idea that property values tend to increase with time, making them a good asset for accumulating wealth. Let's investigate this tactic in greater detail.

The buy-and-hold strategy's fundamental goal is to buy properties with the purpose of holding them for a long time—typically years or even decades. The main objective is to produce rental revenue and enable long-term property appreciation. By keeping ownership, investors can take advantage of the slow rise in property values, which frequently exceeds inflation, as well as the steady income flow from rental payments.

The buy-and-hold strategy's potential for wealth building is one of its main benefits. Properties have a history of long-term appreciation, which can greatly increased an investor's net worth. Furthermore, rental income can generate a consistent flow of passive income, helping to maintain financial stability.

Investors who are successful at buy-and-hold prioritize elements like location, property type, and market trends. They look for homes in places with significant room for expansion, steady employment, and enticing facilities. Additionally, they concentrate on assets that support their investing objectives, be they multi-family, commercial, or residential properties. Risk can be reduced by diversifying a portfolio with a variety of property types.

The buy-and-hold strategy has many advantages, but it also needs persistence, smart property management, and a dedication to long-term objectives. It's a strategy that has proven successful over time and offers a strong foundation for accumulating wealth through real estate, making it an important tool in the investor's toolbox.

Chapter 2: Getting Around the Current Real Estate Scene

The current real estate market is a dynamic and ever-changing ecosystem influenced by a number of variables, such as technology, societal changes, and economic trends. Understanding and adjusting to these developments is crucial for success in the real estate market today.

The impact of technology is one of the most noticeable changes in the current real estate environment. How properties are purchased, sold, and managed has been completely transformed by the internet and digital tools. Real estate searching has become more accessible and practical for both buyers and tenants thanks to online platforms like real estate listing websites and virtual tours. Additionally, data analytics and artificial intelligence have given investors access to insightful information that has enabled them to choose properties and time their investments wisely.

The modern real estate market is significantly shaped by economic changes as well. Interest rates, labor markets, and a region's general economic health all have an impact on market dynamics. Urbanization and demographic changes have recently raised demand for specific property types, such as co-living areas and mixed-use buildings. The importance of sustainability and energy efficiency has increased as people's knowledge of environmental issues has increased.

It's essential for both investors and homeowners to comprehend these patterns. They can use it to find growth possibilities and make wise decisions on whether to acquire, sell, or keep their properties. Adopting a proactive strategy, adopting technology, keeping an eye on market trends, and taking note of tenants' and buyers' evolving tastes are all necessary for success in the modern real estate market.

Individuals can take advantage of these changes when navigating the modern real estate market, whether it is by maximizing property management with smart home technology, investigating emerging markets, or coordinating investments with environmentally friendly and sustainable practices. Investors can take advantage of the possibilities for monetary growth and stability in the current real estate market by adapting to this changing environment.

2.1: Trends and Analysis of the Market

Real estate professionals and investors who are successful use market trends and analysis as a compass. People may make wise judgments, spot opportunities, and successfully negotiate the complexity of the real estate market by comprehending and analyzing these trends.

Monitoring the dynamics of supply and demand is one of the core components of market analysis. Population growth, labor markets, and migration trends are just a few of the variables that affect real estate markets. A growing population frequently causes an increase in housing demand, which may result in price growth. On the other hand, a declining population or economic slump may lead to less demand and thus lower real estate prices. Investors keep an eye on these tendencies to spot markets with promising future growth.

In addition, economic indicators are essential for market analysis. Real estate affordability is influenced by interest rates, inflation, and unemployment rates. While high interest rates might have the opposite impact, low rates can lower borrowing costs and increase demand. Demand for housing may be boosted by a healthy employment market, whereas economic uncertainty may put off prospective tenants or buyers. Investors examine economic data to assess a market's overall health.

Market changes can also have an impact on the types of properties and investment plans. For instance, since individuals prefer larger homes and open areas, the expansion of distant labor during the COVID-19 epidemic has increased interest in suburban and rural properties. The need for warehouses and distribution facilities is influenced by variables like the expansion of e-commerce, which shapes trends in commercial real estate.

Market trends and analysis are essential tools for investors and real estate experts. People can decide when and where to buy, sell, or hold properties by keeping an eye on supply and demand, economic indicators, and changing preferences. Success in the fast-paced real estate industry depends on having a pulse on the market.

2.2: The Effect of Technology on Real Estate

Real estate sector has been irrevocably changed by technology, which has altered how homes are purchased, sold, managed, and even created. The landscape for real estate professionals and customers alike has changed as a result of the digital revolution, which has ushered in an era of ease, efficiency, and accessibility.

The development of online real estate marketplaces is one of the most obvious shifts brought about by technology. Numerous websites and mobile applications, like Zillow, Realtor.com, and Redfin, now offer comprehensive listings, top-notch photographs, virtual tours, and even predictive analytics, making them the go-to sources for real estate searches. Renters and buyers can now research houses from the comfort of their own homes, saving time and travel.

Technology has also streamlined transactional procedures. Remote contract signing has become possible because of electronic signatures, document sharing, and online notaries, which have eliminated the need for in-person meetings and paperwork. By enhancing transparency and lowering fraud, blockchain technology has the potential to completely transform the way people buy and sell properties.

The integration of technology has significantly altered property management as well. Thermostats, security systems, and digital locks are examples of smart home appliances that allow for remote monitoring and control. Rent collection, maintenance requests, and tenant screening are all automated by property management software, making it simpler for landlords to manage their properties effectively.

Technology has made it possible to innovate in the fields of architecture and construction, such as with 3D printing, virtual reality, and building information modeling (BIM). These resources increase project management efficiency, lower costs, and improve design accuracy.

Additionally, for real estate agents, data analytics and artificial intelligence (AI) are now necessary tools. Algorithms powered by AI can be used by investors to forecast market trends and evaluate investment opportunities. In order to maximize rental income and property performance, property managers can examine tenant behavior.

In conclusion, technology has a significant and varied impact on real estate. Property searches have become more accessible thanks to it, and transactions have become more efficient. The real estate sector will undoubtedly continue to change as technology develops, influencing how we buy, sell, and deal with real estate in the future.

Chapter 3: Smart Property Selection

Adopting a wise property selection strategy can have a substantial impact on an investor's long-term financial success. The right property selection is a crucial cornerstone of successful real estate investment. To make sure the chosen property fits with one's investment objectives and has the potential for both growth and consistent returns, this procedure entails a detailed review of a number of different aspects.

The most important consideration in wise property selection is frequently cited as location. The demand for a property and, thus, its potential for appreciation are strongly influenced by the location's desirability. Investors seek out regions with sound economic fundamentals, such as increasing employment, low crime, high-quality public schools, and easy access to services and transportation. The likelihood of future gentrification or development in an area can also be a strong selling point because it may result in rising property values.

The type of property is still another important factor. Each type of property—residential, commercial, and multifamily—has particular benefits and drawbacks. While commercial properties frequently have longer leases and potentially larger yields, residential properties can provide a consistent supply of rental revenue. Apartment buildings and other multi-family structures offer the possibility of diversification within a single asset.

Smart property selection also takes into account the property's condition and room for improvement. An opportunity for value-add investing can arise from a property that requires remodeling or modernization. Investors can save money by buying properties at a lower price, renovating them, and raising the rental income or resale value.

Market research and due diligence are crucial when selecting a home. Investors can make wise judgments by examining current sales data, rental rates, and nearby similar property values. A careful examination of the property can reveal prospective problems or required repairs that might affect the overall profitability of the venture.

In conclusion, selecting a smart property requires careful consideration of the location, type of property, condition, and a detailed market analysis. Investors can position themselves for success and make decisions that are in line with their long-term financial goals by carefully assessing these aspects. Building money through real estate investment requires careful property selection.

3.1: Location

The classic real estate maxim, "Location, location, location," has never been more true. This maxim emphasizes how crucial a property's location is to determining its worth, demand, and investment possibilities. Location is frequently the most crucial element that can make or break an investment in real estate.

The effect of location on demand is one of the main justifications for its importance. Desirable settings tend to attract more prospective purchasers or tenants, such as active metropolitan cores, secure neighborhoods, or regions with top-notch schools and services. In turn, increasing demand may result in higher property values and rental income. On the other hand, properties in less desirable or failing neighborhoods can find it difficult to entice tenants or buyers, thus resulting in poorer returns.

Location must also take accessibility into

consideration. The appeal of a property can be considerably increased by its closeness to major highways, transportation hubs, and public transportation. Accessibility to places for shopping, dining, entertainment, and healthcare can further increase a location's appeal. Properties with connectivity and convenience tend to be more expensive and rentable.

Furthermore, a property's potential for long-term gain is frequently impacted by its location. Property values can rise significantly over time in areas that are undergoing urban development, economic growth, or regeneration activities. Smart investors look for areas with strong growth indicators since these areas are more likely to see capital growth and long-term wealth creation.

While location is crucial, it should not be the only aspect taken into account when making an investment decision. Other factors, like the state of the property, current market conditions, and your investment plan, are also quite important. However, location still serves as the cornerstone of a wise real estate purchase, and grasping its relevance is essential to making decisions that are in line with your financial objectives. It really does come down to location, location, location in the world of real estate.

3.2: Market Niches and Property Types

The choice of real estate types and market niches can have a big impact on an investor's performance in the wide world of real estate investing. This tactical decision entails matching one's investing objectives with the distinctive qualities and prospects of various property classifications.

Residential real estate, which includes single-family homes, condominiums, townhomes, and apartment buildings, is one of the most popular investment options. They frequently offer a consistent flow of rental income and may serve as an ideal starting point for novice investors. For instance, families and people looking for stability and a sense of ownership may find single-family houses appealing. Condos and townhouses can have fewer maintenance requirements, which appeals to busy city dwellers.

There are many different types of commercial

assets, including office buildings, retail establishments, industrial facilities, and warehouses. Each sort of property has a specific function and can meet a range of tenant needs. For example, office spaces are intended for professional services and frequently have long-term lease arrangements. Businesses that depend on foot traffic from customers are housed in retail locations, whereas production and distribution demands are met by industrial buildings.

Apartment complexes and duplexes are examples of multi-family properties that provide the possibility of scalability and diversification within a single investment. These properties have various rental revenue streams, which appeal to investors wishing to diversify their holdings and take advantage of economies of scale. To maintain tenant happiness and retention, they also need efficient property management.

Each property type has certain market niches, which adds another level of complexity and possibility. For instance, niches in the residential sector can be senior living, short-term holiday rentals, or student housing. In the business world, niches can include retail establishments, specialty industrial structures, or medical office buildings.

When choosing property types and niches, successful investors take their investment objectives, risk tolerance, and local market conditions into careful consideration. They may adapt their investments to certain target populations, maximize returns, and minimize potential dangers thanks to this strategic strategy.

In conclusion, selecting the right property types and market niches is a crucial component of real estate investing. It necessitates a thorough comprehension of the distinctive traits and dynamics of each category so that investors may match their selections with their financial goals and build a diverse and potentially profitable portfolio.

Chapter 4: Finance Your Investments

One of the most important steps on the road to financial success is finding the appropriate funding for your real estate projects. Your investment returns, cash flow, and overall profitability can all be dramatically impacted by choosing the correct financing plan.

A home loan is the most typical kind of funding for many investors. By borrowing a sizable amount of the property's purchase price, mortgage finance enables investors to leverage their cash for investment. When interest rates are low, this technique is especially appealing because it may lead to cheaper borrowing costs and maybe higher returns on capital invested.

Depending on their level of risk tolerance and investment objectives, investors can select from a range of mortgage types, such as fixed-rate mortgages, adjustable-rate mortgages, or interest-only loans.

Investors looking for flexibility have more options thanks to innovative financing techniques. In the case of seller financing, the buyer and seller can directly negotiate the terms while the seller serves as the lender. Investors can control a property through lease options without taking instant ownership, giving them the chance to make money from rentals or reserve a property with the intention of buying it later. Alternative methods of funding, frequently with shorter periods and higher interest rates, such as hard money loans and private lending, are available for investors wishing to quickly secure real estate.

The Federal Housing Administration (FHA) and the U.S. Department of Veterans Affairs (VA) both offer financing options that are supported by the government. Real estate investors can also look into these options. For first-time investors or those who meet certain requirements, such as military service, these programs may offer more accessible funding possibilities.

It's important to approach financing with a clear strategy and a complete understanding of the costs, risks, and terms because it can open doors for real estate investing. Investors must also take into account their capacity for managing debt, their ability to pay bills on time, and the possibility of interest rate changes.

In conclusion, choosing how to finance your real estate assets is a crucial choice that has to be well thought out in light of your financial objectives and situation. The capacity to leverage your resources, buy properties, and ultimately create a profitable real estate portfolio can all be improved with the right financing approach. To make sure that your financing decisions match your financial goals and risk tolerance, you must do your research and consult a professional.

4.1: Conventional Financing Alternatives

The foundation of real estate investing has traditionally been traditional financing alternatives, which give investors a dependable way to acquire properties while leveraging their wealth. These traditional techniques are still popular among investors looking for stability and good conditions since they are easily accessible through banks, credit unions, and mortgage lenders.

The conventional mortgage loan is one of the most common types of traditional financing. By paying a down payment and obtaining a loan from a financial institution for the balance of the purchase price, investors can secure a property using this financing method. Investors often select the fixed or adjustable-interest conventional mortgage that best suits their financial objectives and risk tolerance. Homeownership and real estate investing may be more affordable with a reduced down payment, which is typically between 3% and 20% of the property's purchase price.

Home equity loans and lines of credit (HELOC) are two more conventional lending options. These financial tools enable homeowners to fund investment properties by drawing on the equity they've accrued in their principal dwelling. Investors might get a good mortgage rate and terms by using their current home as collateral. Leveraging the value of one property to buy another through home equity financing is a common tactic for growing real estate portfolios.

Strong financial investors may also look at portfolio loans that banks are offering. These loans are designed for people who own several investment properties and might have flexible conditions. In addition to credit ratings and income, they take the borrower's full real estate holdings and financial status into account.

Finally, investors can work with neighborhood community banks or credit unions, which frequently offer individualized service and lending options catered to local market conditions. These organizations might provide affordable rates and a deeper understanding of local real estate dynamics.

Investors can buy real estate assets with the help of solid and readily available traditional financing methods. For investors with solid credit histories and stable finances, these methods frequently provide reasonable interest rates and flexible terms and can be a great option. But in order to make sure that the financing they choose is in line with their investment strategy and long-term objectives, investors must carefully weigh all of their financing options, taking into account things like interest rates, loan terms, and the effect on cash flow.

4.2: Ingenious Financing Techniques

In the field of real estate investing, innovative financing techniques offer many ways to buy properties without relying only on conventional mortgage loans. These novel strategies provide flexibility and may be particularly beneficial for investors dealing with unusual situations or looking for nontraditional investing opportunities.

Seller Financing: Also referred to as owner financing, seller financing enables the seller of the property to act as the lender, thereby lending the buyer the property's purchase price. With adjustable features like interest rates, payback plans, and down payment requirements, this arrangement may be very flexible. For investors who might not be eligible for conventional financing or who want to negotiate unique loan terms with the property seller, seller financing is a compelling alternative.

Lease Options: Leasing gives investors the chance to manage a property without taking direct possession of it. In this deal, the investor leases the asset from the owner with the opportunity to buy it back at a predetermined price within a predetermined time frame. Investors can earn rental income while securing the chance to purchase the property at a later time via lease options. Investors who wish to evaluate a property's potential before buying it may find this tactic useful.

Private lenders and hard money loans: Compared to typical mortgages, private lenders and hard money loans offer financing choices with shorter durations and frequently higher interest rates. Private lenders are people or businesses willing to make loans based on predetermined standards, which may include the investor's background or the worth of the property. Hard money loans are perfect for investors that need immediate access to funds for time-sensitive investments, repairs, or short-term holds because they are often backed by the property itself.

Creative Partnerships: Collaborative financing strategies entail establishing alliances with people or organizations that can contribute money or resources. Examples of these strategies include joint ventures, equity partnerships, or crowdfunding websites. In order to acquire and develop properties, investors may combine their resources with those of partners, sharing the investment's risks and rewards. For bigger or more complicated projects, investors can use creative partnerships to pool resources and skills.

Mortgages with a "wraparound" structure: A wraparound mortgage entails an investor taking over an existing loan and issuing a new mortgage that "wraps around" the original debt. While collecting payments from the buyer of the property at a higher interest rate, the investor pays payments to the initial lender. This tactic can be applied to increase revenue and leverage an existing loan.

Innovative financing techniques enable investors to think creatively and customize their finances to fit particular investment conditions. These techniques may have particular benefits, but they also have certain hazards and difficulties, so they must be used with caution. In order to develop broad portfolios and take advantage of opportunities that match their investing aims, successful investors frequently blend traditional and innovative financing strategies.

Chapter 5: Smart Property Management

In today's digital age, implementing smart property management methods can dramatically improve an investor's capacity to maximize returns and streamline operations. Successful real estate investing is largely dependent on efficient property management. Utilizing cutting-edge tactics and technology to maximize a property's performance, improve the tenant experience, and ultimately increase revenue is known as smart property management.

The incorporation of smart home technology is one of the essential elements of smart property management. Smart locks, thermostats, and security systems are examples of Internet of Things (IoT) products that allow for remote monitoring and control. These technologies can help investors increase energy efficiency, increase security, and promptly respond to maintenance needs. Smart home technologies can also increase a property's appeal to tech-savvy tenants, thereby boosting rental revenue and asset value.

Another crucial tool in the toolbox of a savvy property manager is property management software. Numerous processes, including rent collection, lease management, maintenance tracking, and tenant interactions, are automated by these platforms. Property managers can lower administrative costs, cut down on errors, and boost overall operational effectiveness by optimizing these operations. These platforms also offer insightful data analytics, empowering investors to make data-driven choices to maximize the performance of real estate.

A key component of wise property management is effective tenant communication. Digital channels can be used by property managers to expedite communication, fix issues, and offer timely updates, such as email, text messaging, and tenant portals. Retention rates and tenant satisfaction are strongly related, and effective communication can result in longer tenant stays and shorter vacancy times.

Proactive maintenance methods are also crucial for effective property management. Using data from the Internet of Things and routine property inspections, investors can develop preventive maintenance regimens. Property managers may lower repair costs, increase the longevity of property systems, and improve tenant satisfaction by resolving problems before they worsen.

In conclusion, smart property management integrates automation, technology, and proactive measures to improve tenant satisfaction and optimize property performance. In an increasingly competitive real estate market, investors that adopt these strategies will be better able to maximize their profits, minimize operational inefficiencies, and preserve long-term profitability.

5.1: Best Practices for Property Management

Maintaining the value of real estate assets and ensuring tenants have a great experience depend on effective property management. Best practices for property management cover a wide range of tactics and ideas that support long-term financial success and asset protection for investors.

Thorough tenant screening is one of the foundational elements of effective property management. Finding trustworthy and accountable tenants is made easier by doing thorough background investigations, which also include credit checks, rental history inquiries, and criminal background checks. By doing this, the chance of late payments, property damage, and eviction actions is reduced.

Regular Property Inspections: It's important to conduct regular property inspections to spot maintenance issues as soon as they arise. Property managers can quickly address damages thanks to routine inspections, which keep the building in good shape and preserve its value.

Clear Lease Agreements: A successful property management strategy is built on carefully designed lease agreements. All terms and conditions, such as rent payment dates, obligations for maintenance and repairs, and guidelines for tenant behavior, should be outlined in these agreements. Lease agreement clarity helps prevent misunderstandings and disagreements.

Maintenance that is prompt and responsive is essential for tenant satisfaction. Tenants should have a procedure for reporting maintenance issues, and property managers should make sure that these issues are resolved quickly. Additionally, regular preventative maintenance can lower repair costs and extend the lifespan of building systems.

Effective Communication: Keeping good relationships with tenants requires open and efficient communication. The mechanisms through which renters can report issues or ask for repairs should be made clear by property managers. Additionally, it promotes trust and transparency to keep tenants informed about significant property-related issues like rent increases or rule changes.

Financial management: Property managers need to keep up-to-date budgets and financial records. Investors can evaluate the financial performance of their properties and make wise decisions by keeping track of income and expenses. Putting money aside to cover unforeseen costs is also a wise idea.

Legal Compliance: Property managers are required to keep abreast of all applicable local, state, and federal rules and regulations. To minimize legal problems and potential liabilities, it is essential to comply with regulations governing landlord-tenant relationships, tenant rights, and fair housing.

Tenant Retention: It's frequently less expensive to keep dependable tenants than to search for new ones. Longer tenancy lengths and lower vacancy rates can be achieved by providing incentives for lease renewals and immediately resolving tenant complaints.

Technology Integration: Using technology, such as smart home gadgets and property management software, helps streamline processes and increase efficiency. These solutions can automate communication, maintenance requests, and rent collection, improving the effectiveness of property management.

In conclusion, sustaining real estate investments is covered in detail by best practices for property management. Property managers may safeguard property values, foster a welcoming atmosphere for tenants, and ultimately contribute to long-term success in the real estate market by putting a priority on tenant screening, regular inspections, clear communication, and proactive upkeep.

5.2: Using Technology to Increase Efficiency

Technology has developed into a potent ally for real estate professionals who want to increase productivity, streamline procedures, and streamline their business operations in the current era. Leveraging technological breakthroughs has completely changed how real estate is maintained, advertised, and traded, providing several advantages to buyers, sellers, and agents.

Property Management Software: The way properties are managed has changed as a result of property management software platforms. Property managers can automate a variety of duties with the help of these technologies, such as rent collection, lease administration, maintenance requests, and tenant communications. Property managers can lessen administrative work, cut down on mistakes, and boost operational effectiveness by automating these activities. These platforms also offer insightful data analytics, empowering investors to make data-driven choices to maximize the performance of real estate.

Technology for Smart Homes: The use of smart house technology has altered the field of property management. Smart locks, security systems, and thermostats are examples of Internet of Things (IoT) devices that allow for remote monitoring and control. These technologies can help property managers and landlords increase energy efficiency, increase security, and swiftly address maintenance needs. Smart home technologies can also increase a property's appeal to tech-savvy tenants, thereby boosting rental revenue and asset value.

Online listing and marketing platforms: More online listing and marketing platforms than ever before are available to real estate professionals. These platforms also reach a much wider audience. Predictive analytics, extensive property listings, top-notch photographs, and virtual tours are all available on websites and mobile apps. These platforms enable property managers, agents, and investors to efficiently market properties, luring potential tenants and buyers with accessibility and convenience.

Digital Transactions: The purchasing and selling of real estate have become more effective as a result of the digitization of these transactions. Remote contract signing has become possible because of electronic signatures, document sharing, and online notaries, which have eliminated the need for in-person meetings and paperwork. By enhancing transparency and eliminating fraud, blockchain technology has the ability to completely transform the way that people buy and sell properties.

AI and Data Analytics: For real estate professionals, AI and data analytics have become indispensable tools. Algorithms powered by AI can be used by investors to forecast market trends and evaluate investment opportunities. In order to maximize rental income and property performance, property managers can examine tenant behavior. Professionals may now make well-informed decisions and quickly adjust to shifting market situations thanks to these technologies.

In conclusion, success in the contemporary real

estate sector is now characterized by the effective use of technology. Real estate agents may operate more efficiently, provide better service to their clients, and maintain competition in a market that is changing quickly by embracing property management software, smart home technologies, online marketing, digital transactions, and data analytics. These technical developments have changed the industry and will likely continue to do so.

Chapter 6: Building Your Real Estate Portfolio

Creating a real estate portfolio is a calculated move that can result in wealth creation and long-term financial success. The process of building a portfolio requires careful planning, investment techniques, and a clear grasp of your financial goals, whether you are a newbie investor or a seasoned professional.

Establish Your Investment Goals: Setting your investment goals is the first step in creating a real estate portfolio. Are you searching for long-term growth, consistent rental income, or a combination of both? Do you want to specialize in a certain property type or market niche? Or perhaps you want to diversify your stock portfolio.

Your investment approach will be guided by your goals, which will also enable you to make wise choices.

Prior to beginning any real estate investments, it is essential to evaluate your financial situation. Analyze your financial resources to see how much you can comfortably invest in real estate and how much is accessible for other assets. Examine your capacity for risk and, if necessary, your ability to secure funding.

Start Small and Learn: It's advised to start small and get experience if you're new to real estate investment. Think about making your initial investments in single-family homes or modest multi-family buildings. This enables you to handle the properties while learning the ropes and comprehending local market dynamics.

Diversify Your Portfolio: When establishing a portfolio, diversification is a key component. Diversify your investment portfolio by investing in various markets, property types, and geographical regions. As markets fluctuate, diversification can help reduce risk and offer stability.

Conduct Thorough Due Diligence: Before purchasing any property, careful due diligence is required. Investigate the market circumstances, evaluate property values, and comprehend the rental market in your area. Carefully examine properties to find any problems that might reduce their worth or rental revenue.

Use leverage sensibly. Leveraging can be a potent instrument for portfolio expansion. Consider using leverage to buy multiple properties if you have access to mortgage loans or other sources of funding. However, proceed with caution, taking into account both your capacity for managing debt and the risks involved.

Focus on Property Management: The success of a portfolio depends on effective property management. Implement effective property management techniques, such as streamlining operations with smart home technologies and property management software. Longer tenancies and reduced vacancy rates might result from offering exceptional tenant experiences.

Monitor and Modify: Continue to keep an eye on how your properties and portfolio as a whole are performing. Keep an eye on rental revenue, spending, and market changes. Be ready to modify your plan as necessary to keep up with shifting market conditions or your evolving financial objectives.

Seek Expert Advice: Creating a real estate portfolio can be challenging, so consulting real estate experts, financial consultants, or mentors can be quite beneficial. You may negotiate the complexity of real estate investment with the support of professionals who can provide insights, advice, and strategies.

Finally, creating a real estate portfolio is a dynamic process that calls for meticulous preparation, diligence, and a long-term outlook. You may slowly expand your portfolio and work toward attaining your financial goals in the world of real estate investment with a clear grasp of your goals, strong financial management, and a dedication to ongoing learning and adaptation.

6.1: Scaling Your Investments

Scaling your real estate assets entails extending your exposure to the real estate market and diversifying your portfolio of properties. For investors hoping to increase their wealth and produce significant passive income, it's a crucial step. Key factors to keep in mind for scaling real estate investing techniques are as follows:

Leverage Equity: Using the equity in your current properties is one of the most popular strategies to increase the size of your real estate assets. You accumulate equity as time passes, the value of your house rises, and your mortgage balance falls. By refinancing or obtaining home equity loans, you can use this equity to pay for the purchase of other homes.

Access to Funding: Scaling frequently necessitates securing funding in addition to your initial cash. As your portfolio expands, think about your capacity to get home loans, business loans, or other types of finance. You may be able to get better financing terms if you establish solid credit, keep a clean financial record, and have a history of profitable investments.

Diversification: Spreading your real estate assets over various property types, markets, or geographical areas can lower risk and increase the stability of your portfolio. Consider expanding into regions or property types that fit your investing objectives and present expansion potential.

Joint ventures and partnerships: Forming partnerships or joint ventures might be a smart way to grow. Partnerships can give you access to more money, knowledge, and resources. It's crucial to have precise agreements and comparable investment objectives when forming partnerships.

Professional Property Management: As your

business grows, effective property management becomes more and more important. The use of property management software and professional property management techniques can help improve tenant satisfaction by streamlining operations and lowering management costs.

Market research: Thorough market research becomes crucial when increasing your investments. The markets, trends, and growth prospects in the areas where you plan to invest should all be evaluated. Your growth choices might be influenced by keeping up with local changes, job markets, and economic data.

Risk management: Risk management gets increasingly complicated as you scale. A thorough risk management strategy that includes insurance coverage, backup plans, and cash reserves for unforeseen costs or market downturns is essential.

Portfolio optimization: Consistently analyze the performance of your current portfolio and determine whether it is aligned with your objectives. Selling underperforming investments or investments that no longer suit your investment strategy could help you maximize your portfolio.

Continued Learning: In order to scale your investments, you might need to adjust to new possibilities and difficulties. Continue to gain knowledge of real estate markets, investing methods, and market trends. Insights can be gained from networking and professional growth within the real estate industry.

Scaling your real estate assets is a dynamic process that calls for careful planning, sound financial judgment, and a readiness to change course when necessary. You can successfully expand your investments and work toward attaining your long-term financial goals in the real estate market by using strong financial practices, strategically diversifying, and being educated.

6.2: Diversification Techniques

A key tactic for reducing risk and maximizing returns in a real estate investment portfolio is diversification. Investors can lessen their exposure to the volatility of any one asset or location by spreading their assets across many property types, geographic regions, and marketplaces. Key diversification tactics to think about are listed below:

Diversification of Property Types: There is some risk mitigation when investing in different kinds of properties. Commercial, industrial, and multifamily properties all have different risk and return profiles. The performance of the portfolio can be balanced by diversifying among various sectors.

Market diversification can reduce the risk brought on by local economic downturns or market-specific issues by investing in a variety of markets or geographies. While one market may fail, another might prosper, stabilizing the portfolio as a whole. Think about cities with a variety of sectors and strong economies.

Diversification of Investment Strategies: There are various ways to invest in real estate, including buy-and-hold, fix-and-flip, and short-term rentals. By utilizing a variety of investment strategies, investors can profit from changing market dynamics and possible gains. For instance, fix-and-flip methods prioritize quick profits, while buy-and-hold strategies offer long-term stability.

Diversifying your holdings across several asset classes could include investing in real estate investment trusts (REITs) or real estate crowdfunding websites. These investments can offer liquidity and diversification advantages while providing exposure to real estate markets without direct property ownership.

Goals and Risk Tolerance: Diversification techniques should be in line with the financial goals and risk tolerance of an investor. While investors expecting greater profits might look into development projects or commercial real estate, those seeking a steady income might prefer residential rentals. Diversification must be tailored to each person's goals.

Professional property management is crucial for portfolios with a variety of investments. Property managers are skilled at handling the subtle differences between various property kinds and markets, ensuring that assets are efficiently managed, renters are happy, and income is maximized.

Monitoring on an ongoing basis: Diversification shouldn't be a one-time endeavor. Keep a close eye on the performance of your portfolio and evaluate how well it fits with your goals. Diversification tactics should be adjusted when market conditions or your goals change.

Real estate investment diversification is a dynamic strategy that adapts to shifting market conditions and personal investment goals. Investors may create robust portfolios that are better able to withstand market volatility and optimize long-term returns while effectively managing risk by carefully planning and putting diversification strategies into place.

Chapter 7: Legal and Risk Management Considerations

In order to invest successfully in real estate, one must have a thorough awareness of the risks involved as well as the relevant legal issues. To protect your investments and ensure legal compliance, it's essential to manage these components. These are significant considerations:

Due Diligence: The cornerstone of risk management in real estate is thorough due diligence. Make thorough inquiries and inspections before purchasing any property. This includes examining the property's state, going over its financial background, and determining the stability of the neighborhood market. Making educated investment selections is possible when potential problems are identified beforehand.

Financial Risk: Investing in real estate frequently requires substantial outlays of cash. Before you make any investments, consider your financial situation and risk tolerance. Take into account aspects like property financing, property maintenance fees, and the possibility of unforeseen charges. Cash risks can be reduced by creating cash reserves and backup plans.

Market Risk: Economic, demographic, and sector-specific factors all have an impact on the real estate market's cyclical nature. The possibility of falling property values or falling rental demand are examples of market risk. Your portfolio's diversification across several markets and property types might help reduce market risk.

Legal Compliance: It's crucial to abide by all applicable local, state, and federal rules and regulations. Real estate investments are impacted by tax laws, zoning rules, landlord-tenant laws, and fair housing laws. To ensure complete legal compliance and reduce legal risks, consult with legal professionals or seek guidance from specialists.

Contracts and Agreements: Several contracts and agreements are involved in real estate transactions. These agreements, including purchase agreements, leasing agreements, and finance contracts, should be carefully reviewed and negotiated. A well-written and transparent contract can safeguard your interests and lower legal risks.

Property Insurance: Sufficient property insurance is necessary to reduce the risk of liability or property damage. To protect your assets and investments, take into account several insurance choices, such as property insurance, liability insurance, and landlord insurance.

Expert Advice: When investing in real estate, expert advice is frequently beneficial. Think about collaborating with real estate-focused financial advisors, property managers, and attorneys. You can handle challenging legal and financial issues with their experience.

Strategies for Managing Risk: Create risk management plans that are suited to your investing goals. These can include diversifying your investment portfolio, saving aside funds for unforeseen costs, and putting preventative maintenance procedures in place to lessen the risk of expensive repairs.

Continuous Monitoring: Risk management is a lifelong process. Keep an eye on your investments and stay up-to-date on any changes to the laws, regulations, and business climate in your area. Be prepared to adjust your strategy when circumstances change.

In conclusion, successful real estate investment depends on risk management and legal concerns. Investors can reduce possible risks and safeguard their investments in a dynamic and ever-changing real estate market by performing extensive due diligence, guaranteeing legal compliance, and putting into practice effective risk management measures.

7.1: Risk Reduction for Investments

Successful real estate investing fundamentally involves minimizing investment risks. Real estate has inherent dangers in addition to the potential for significant rewards. The following are crucial tactics for reducing these risks:

Diversification: This is a key component of risk reduction. Reduce your exposure to the volatility of any one asset or location by diversifying your assets among many property kinds, regions, and markets. The risk and return profile of your portfolio can be balanced by diversification.

Thorough Due Diligence: Before purchasing any property, thorough due diligence must be performed. Examine property valuations, market circumstances, and rental demand in your area. Carefully examine properties to find any problems that might reduce their worth or rental revenue.

Financial research: Conduct in-depth financial research to make sure your investments match your risk tolerance and financial goals. Take into account elements including finance for the property, running costs, possible rental income, and cash flow estimates. Evaluate your capacity to withstand financial hardships or unforeseen costs.

Risk evaluation: Identify and evaluate any possible hazards that are unique to your assets. Market risk, property condition risk, tenant-related risk, and finance risk are a few examples. You can create methods to reduce risks by having a thorough understanding of the risks related to each investment.

Maintaining liquidity will allow you to cover unforeseen costs and seize investment possibilities. You can handle financial difficulties without endangering your investments if you have cash reserves or access to funding.

Professional Advice: Consult with real estate experts, financial consultants, and attorneys who focus on real estate investment for guidance. These experts can offer insightful advice, guide you through challenging legal and financial issues, and guarantee that you make well-informed decisions.

Strategies for Managing Risk: Create risk management plans that are suited to your investing goals. For instance, put in place insurance policies to guard against unanticipated events or establish preventative maintenance procedures to lower property-related risks.

Legal Compliance: Adhere to all applicable laws and rules. Verify that the zoning rules, tax codes, landlord-tenant legislation, and fair housing laws are followed by your investments. Compliance with the law reduces legal risks while also defending your standing as an investor.

Continuous monitoring is necessary for effective risk reduction. Keep a close eye on the markets, the economy, and your investments. Be prepared to adjust your strategy when circumstances change.

In conclusion, real estate investment risk mitigation calls for a multi-pronged strategy that combines diversification, meticulous due diligence, financial analysis, expert counsel, and constant monitoring. Investors can improve their capacity to manage risk successfully and realize their long-term investment objectives by putting these tactics into practice and keeping themselves updated on market conditions.

7.2: Compliance and Legal Aspects

To secure their assets and uphold moral and legal standards, investors in real estate must traverse a challenging legal environment. A successful real estate investment journey requires an understanding of and adherence to different legal requirements:

Contracts and Agreements: Several contracts and agreements, including purchase contracts, leasing agreements, and financing paperwork, are frequently used in real estate transactions. In order to safeguard your interests and make sure that all parties' obligations are clearly specified, it is essential to carefully analyze, negotiate, and comprehend these contracts.

Title and Ownership: A title search is necessary to confirm the ownership of the property and to find out if there are any liens, encumbrances, or legal difficulties that might limit the property's marketability. It's essential to resolve title difficulties before concluding any real estate deal.

Zoning and land use restrictions: The way that properties can be utilized and developed is determined by local zoning laws and land use restrictions. To make sure that their proposed use of the property complies with regional legislation, investors must be aware of these rules. In some circumstances, requesting zoning variances or approvals may be required.

Understanding landlord-tenant rules, which vary by jurisdiction, is crucial if you intend to lease your property. The management of security deposits, eviction procedures, and lease conditions are all governed by these regulations. Financial obligations and legal issues may result from non-compliance.

Fair housing regulations: These regulations forbid discrimination in housing on the basis of race, ethnicity, religion, national origin, sex, disability, and family status. All facets of real estate administration, such as tenant screening, lease agreements, and property upkeep, require investors to abide by these rules.

Environmental Rules: Properties may be subject to environmental rules pertaining to things like wetlands, contaminants, and dangerous chemicals. When appropriate, investors should perform environmental assessments and adhere to environmental regulations, including disclosure obligations.

Tax implications for real estate investments include capital gains taxes, income taxes, and property taxes. Investors can improve their tax strategy and reduce tax liabilities by being aware of the tax code and the available deductions.

Regulations pertaining to financing and mortgages: Investors who use finance for real estate investments are required to adhere to the rules pertaining to financing and mortgages. In order to avoid legal problems, it is crucial to understand the terms and conditions of mortgage loans.

Professional Advice: Due to the complexity of the legal elements of real estate, it is strongly advised that you seek the advice of a real estate law specialist. Lawyers can represent your interests in court, evaluate contracts, verify compliance, and offer helpful counsel.

Continuous Compliance: Maintaining legal compliance requires constant effort. Property owners and investors need to be aware of any modifications to the laws, rules, and industry standards that may have an effect on their investments. It is crucial to regularly examine and update lease agreements and property management procedures.

In conclusion, understanding the legal ramifications and compliance needs of real estate investing is essential for safeguarding your capital, upholding moral principles, and averting pricey legal fights. Investors can reduce legal risks and guarantee a smooth and successful investment journey by prioritizing legal diligence and seeking professional help as needed.

Chapter 8: Increasing Returns with Innovation

Innovation is crucial to real estate investing because it creates new opportunities for increasing profits and efficiency. Investors that adopt cutting-edge strategies can gain a competitive advantage and seize chances that conventional tactics might miss. Here are some strategies for utilizing innovation to increase real estate returns:

Integration of Technology: The real estate sector has undergone a change. Investors can expedite processes, improve tenant experiences, and maximize rental income with the use of property management software, data analytics, and smart home technology. Investors can make wise selections because of these innovations' useful insights into things like market trends and metrics measuring the performance of properties.

Crowdfunding and online platforms: By enabling investors to combine their funds and take part in bigger projects, real estate crowdfunding platforms have democratized real estate investment. These platforms open up a variety of investing opportunities, frequently with reduced entrance requirements. By spreading their money over several projects, investors can lower their risk and possibly increase their returns.

Blockchain and tokenization: Real estate assets are being tokenized using blockchain technology, allowing for fractional ownership and increased liquidity. Tokenization makes it simpler for investors to diversify their portfolios and access formerly illiquid assets by allowing them to buy and sell shares in properties. By increasing market involvement, this innovation increases flexibility and has the potential to produce higher returns.

Making Data-Driven Decisions: Artificial intelligence and data analytics enable investors to make data-driven decisions. Investors can find investment possibilities, maximize rental revenue, and reduce risks by studying market data, tenant behavior, and property performance measures. These revelations help us make better-informed investing decisions.

Green and sustainable investments: Eco-friendly and sustainable methods are becoming more and more significant in the real estate industry. In addition to aligning with environmental goals, investments in green technologies or energy-efficient buildings also draw in environmentally conscientious tenants. Sustainable design elements can save costs and possibly increase rental income, increasing overall returns.

Vacation homes and short-term rentals: Websites like Airbnb have changed the short-term rental industry. By focusing on leisure and business visitors, investors can take advantage of these platforms to increase returns. To maximize short-term rental income, it is crucial to comprehend regional laws and market trends.

Repurposing existing assets through adaptive reuse or redevelopment can create a considerable return on investment. Modernizing outmoded or unused buildings into residential, commercial, or mixed-use areas can increase rental income and increase the value of the property.

Proptech Startups and Innovations: Keep up with the latest developments in the field. These businesses frequently present cutting-edge approaches to marketing, investment research, tenant screening, and property management. A competitive edge might be gained by investigating partnerships or investments in proptech.

In conclusion, innovation in real estate investing presents chances to boost profits, lower risk, and maintain competitiveness in a fast-moving market. Investors can use innovation to increase the profitability of their real estate portfolios by adopting data-driven methods, embracing new investing platforms, and embracing technology.

8.1: Innovations in Real Estate Technology

The way that investors, buyers, sellers, and property managers conduct business is changing as a result of technological advancements in the real estate sector. These developments are strengthening not only efficiency but also the entire real estate experience.

1. Property Management Software: For investors and property managers, property management software has changed the game. Tasks like rent collection, maintenance requests, lease management, and tenant communication are made easier by these platforms. Real-time data, analytics, and automation are all available to property managers, increasing productivity and tenant satisfaction.

2. Smart Home Technology: The incorporation of smart home gadgets improves the efficiency and appeal of real estate. Investors are outfitting properties with Internet of Things (IoT) gadgets that enable remote monitoring and management, such as smart locks, security systems, and thermostats. In addition to increasing property value, this technology also enables energy savings and increased security.

3. Virtual and augmented reality: These two types of technology are revolutionizing the way people view properties. Now, from the convenience of their homes, buyers and investors may take virtual tours of properties. By decreasing the need for in-person visits and speeding up the property search process, this technology benefits all parties.

4. Blockchain and tokenization: Through tokenization, blockchain technology is gaining traction in the real estate sector. This invention makes real estate investments more accessible to a wider variety of investors by allowing for fractional ownership of buildings. Blockchain also increases confidence and transparency in real estate transactions by decreasing fraud.

5. Real estate crowdsourcing: Crowdfunding websites have made real estate investing more accessible. Smaller capital contributions from investors might be pooled to finance larger real estate developments. More people can engage in the real estate market because of this innovation's increased investment thresholds and prospects for diversification.

6. Artificial intelligence and predictive analytics: Real estate is using data-driven decision-making more and more. By examining market trends, data on property performance, and tenant behavior, artificial intelligence and predictive analytics assist investors and property managers in making wise decisions. More precise pricing, risk assessment, and investment strategy optimization are made possible by this technology.

7. Online listing platforms for properties: These platforms are now the main means by which properties are advertised and found. To aid buyers and investors in making wise choices, these websites offer thorough property information, high-quality photos, and even predictive analytics. The ease of web listings has completely changed the way people look for properties.

8. Green and sustainable technologies: Sustainability is a developing trend in the real estate industry. By making investments in energy-efficient real estate, renewable energy sources, and green technologies, investors are embracing environmentally beneficial activities. These eco-friendly features not only lower operating expenses but also draw tenants who care about the environment, which could increase rental income.

In conclusion, technological advancements in real estate are transforming the sector and benefiting buyers, sellers, investors, and property managers greatly. These developments are raising property values, streamlining processes, increasing efficiency, and making real estate investments more accessible and sustainable than ever. Anyone working in the real estate industry needs to stay current on these technical developments.

8.2: Green and sustainable investing

As environmental knowledge and eco-consciousness continue to rise, sustainable and green real estate investing have become increasingly popular. This strategy involves integrating environmentally friendly methods and technologies into real estate investments, and it provides both investors and the environment with a number of advantages:

Sustainable real estate investments frequently place a high priority on energy efficiency. Energy consumption and operating costs are reduced in buildings with energy-efficient HVAC, lighting, and appliances. Properties that have lower utility costs are more appealing to renters, which increases rental income and increases the value of the property.

Renewable Energy: Property owners can increase their revenue by investing in renewable energy sources like solar or wind power. Investors can lessen their carbon footprint and generate a new source of income by producing renewable energy and selling excess electricity back to the grid.

Green building certifications: homes that have earned LEED (Leadership in Energy and Environmental Design) or ENERGY STAR certifications typically have higher rentals and property values. These accreditations imply a dedication to excellence and sustainability, luring investors and tenants who care about the environment.

Waste Reduction: Through recycling initiatives and effective waste management systems, sustainable properties seek to reduce waste. In addition to helping the environment, trash reduction also lowers disposal costs and enhances the appearance of real estate.

Water conservation is made possible on sustainable properties through irrigation systems, water-wise landscaping, and fixtures. Lower utility costs are produced by using less water, which is in line with the rising worries about a water shortage.

Sustainable buildings put a priority on indoor air quality by using low-VOC (volatile organic compound) paints, non-toxic materials, and enough ventilation. The satisfaction and wellbeing of tenants are influenced by healthy indoor settings.

Tax advantages and incentives: Many governments provide tax breaks and credits for environmentally friendly real estate developments. The initial expenses of adopting green technologies and practices can be greatly decreased by these financial incentives.

Eco-Friendly Amenities: Sustainable homes frequently have environmentally friendly features like bike parking, EV charging stations, and green roofs. These characteristics increase the property's appeal and draw environmentally conscious tenants.

Long-Term Investment: Green and sustainable investments are frequently thought of as long-term projects. Eco-friendly features' robustness and energy efficiency can eventually result in lower maintenance costs, boosting the property's potential long-term viability and returns.

Alignment with Values: Sustainable and green investing enable people and businesses to link their financial decisions with their moral and ethical principles. It generates profits while giving one the satisfaction of helping to create a more sustainable future.

In conclusion, sustainable and green real estate investing is a progressive strategy that is advantageous to both investors and the environment. In addition to solving significant environmental concerns, it can result in cost savings, higher property prices, and improved tenant satisfaction. These investments are probably going to become more appealing and profitable as sustainability continues to gain importance.

Chapter 9: Wealth Preservation and Exit Strategies

In order to invest successfully in real estate, one must not only buy properties but also make future plans, such as how to sell holdings and protect wealth. For risk management and return maximization, it is crucial to implement effective exit strategies:

1. Selling for Capital Gains: Selling real estate for capital gains is a frequent departure strategy. When property values have dramatically increased, investors could decide to sell so they can make a profit. Strategic sales can result in significant returns, but timing is also very important.

2. Long-Term Rentals: Maintaining properties as long-term rentals can generate a consistent flow of rental income and create wealth over the long term. Investors can profit from current cash flow and potential future property appreciation with this technique.

3. 1031 Exchange: A 1031 exchange enables investors to sell one property and reinvest the proceeds into another of equal or better worth. It is a tax-deferred method. By delaying capital gains taxes and enabling investment returns to accumulate, this tactic can aid in wealth preservation.

4. Selling a section of a property while keeping ownership of the rest is an option for investors. With this strategy, it is possible to realize some gains while still owning a portion of the property that can continue to bring in rental revenue.

5. Refinancing: Investors can access equity while still owning a property by refinancing it. Investors can use the money freed up by a favorable refinance to make additional investments or improvements to existing properties, thereby raising rental revenue and property value.

6. Estate Planning: For the purpose of preserving wealth, estate planning is essential. Investors can design estate plans that specify how real estate holdings will be passed on to heirs, potentially reducing estate taxes and guaranteeing a seamless transfer of wealth to the following generation.

7. Portfolio Diversification: Increasing portfolio diversity can lower risk and improve wealth preservation. Investment diversification across several asset classes, markets, and property types can offer stability amid market turbulence.

8. Professional Advice: When thinking about departure alternatives, consulting with financial consultants, tax experts, and real estate specialists is crucial. Professionals can assist investors in developing a customized exit strategy, navigating intricate tax ramifications, and evaluating market circumstances.

9. Monitoring market movements: Successful exits depend on keeping a close eye on real estate market movements. Investors should be ready to modify their exit strategies in response to shifting economic data, demand trends, and market conditions.

10. Tax Efficiency: One of the most important aspects of asset preservation is minimizing tax payments. To maximize their financial outcomes, investors should look into tax-efficient measures, including deferring capital gains, tax credits, or deductions.

Finally, preparing wealth preservation and exit strategies is essential to real estate investing success. Investors should carefully evaluate their financial objectives, the state of the market, and the tax ramifications of several exit strategies. Investors can take proactive steps to preserve their wealth and find competent advice, enabling them to make decisions that are in line with their long-term financial goals.

9.1: Strategically Marketing Your Real Estate

Real estate investing requires a systematic approach to selling properties because it can have a big impact on profits and financial objectives. In order to streamline the selling process, investors must take into account a number of variables and employ practical strategies, such as:

Market timing: To maximize returns, the market must be timed. Investors should keep an eye on the situation of their local real estate markets, including changes in supply and demand, interest rates, and economic indicators. When supply is limited and demand is high, selling might result in higher sale prices.

Property Condition: For properties to attract buyers and increase value, they must be presented in the best possible condition. To boost curb appeal and overall property beauty, take into account making the necessary repairs, renovations, and aesthetic enhancements. Additionally, staging might aid prospective buyers in seeing the potential of the property.

Pricing Strategy: Choosing the appropriate listing price is important. Underpricing may result in lost profit chances, while overpricing may result in extended market time and eventual price reductions. To determine similar property values and establish a reasonable price, perform a comparative market analysis (CMA).

Marketing and Exposure: To reach a larger audience of potential customers, a thorough marketing strategy is essential. To highlight the features of the home, make use of both conventional and modern marketing techniques, such as real estate listings, social media, expert photography, and virtual tours.

Professional Representation: Working with a knowledgeable real estate broker or agent can provide you access to their knowledge of pricing, marketing, and negotiating. An experienced agent can help you efficiently navigate the selling process and guide you in making wise decisions.

Pre-Sale Inspections: By performing pre-sale inspections, any problems that can emerge during the selling process can be found. The likelihood of a smooth transaction can be increased by proactively addressing these difficulties in order to avoid surprises and delays.

Negotiation Approach: Be ready to haggle with prospective purchasers. Examine offers thoroughly, taking into account the terms and contingencies in addition to the sale price. An advantageous sale may result from a carefully considered bargaining strategy.

Tax Implications: Recognize how selling a property will affect your taxes, particularly any capital gains taxes. Tax effects may differ depending on the holding duration, if the property is a principal residence, and other elements. Consult a tax expert to investigate tax-saving options.

If you intend to buy real estate again after selling, think about a 1031 exchange. By investing the proceeds in a property of a similar type, you can use this tax-deferred technique to postpone paying capital gains taxes.

Have backup plans in place in case of unforeseen events like problems with the buyer's finances, problematic inspection findings, or inconsistent appraisal results. Deals falling through can be avoided by being ready to handle these difficulties.

Closure procedure: There are a number of formal and procedural steps involved in the closure procedure. To ensure a successful closing, make sure all required paperwork is in place and that you are ready to collaborate closely with escrow agents, title companies, and lawyers.

In conclusion, rigorous preparation, market research, and close attention to detail are necessary for strategic selling in real estate. Investors can maximize returns and meet their financial objectives when selling properties by taking into account variables such as market timing, property quality, pricing, and marketing. A successful sales strategy relies on expert advice and proactive planning.

9.2: Planning a legacy to preserve wealth

A comprehensive strategy for wealth preservation and smooth wealth transfer to future generations is called legacy planning. Legacy planning is essential in real estate investment, where significant assets are frequently at stake, to protect the financial stability of heirs and beneficiaries. Considerations for legacy planning include the following:

Estate Planning: The foundation of legacy planning is estate planning. It entails drafting a legally binding plan for how your assets, including real estate, will be distributed after your death. Documents like wills, trusts, and powers of attorney often fall into this category. Real estate assets are allocated in accordance with your intentions and in a tax-effective way thanks to estate planning.

Tax Efficiency: When sold or inherited, real estate investments may have tax ramifications. Legacy planning tries to reduce tax obligations for recipients and heirs. To lower inheritance and capital gains taxes, strategies like gifting, family limited partnerships, and trusts can be used.

Asset protection is a component of legacy planning that includes methods for shielding real estate assets from heirs' potential financial difficulties, lawsuits, and creditors. While retaining authority over the properties, using legal frameworks like trusts can provide asset protection.

Succession Planning: A succession plan is necessary if you want to pass on real estate interests to family members or company partners. To ensure that the real estate portfolio continues to succeed, clearly define the roles, responsibilities, and decision-making procedures for the following generation.

Property Management: Future property management of real estate properties should be considered in legacy planning. Think about whether the heirs have the skills and knowledge to handle the properties themselves or whether hiring a property management company is necessary.

Philanthropic Objectives: Many people include philanthropy in their legacy planning by allocating a percentage of their money to foundations or charitable organizations. Real estate assets can be contributed to nonprofits, providing tax advantages and helping to leave a lasting legacy of philanthropy.

Open Communication: Open communication with beneficiaries and heirs is essential to successful legacy planning. To prevent disagreements or misunderstandings, discuss your intentions, objectives, and plans concerning real estate holdings with your family or beneficiaries.

Advice from a professional: Legacy planning in real estate can be complicated and involve legal, financial, and tax issues. You can negotiate the complexities of legacy planning and make sure that your preferences are accurately recorded and carried out by seeking the advice of attorneys, financial consultants, and estate planners who specialize in real estate.

Regular Review: Estate plans shouldn't be rigid; they should be responsive to changing conditions. Review your plan on a regular basis, especially following big life occurrences like births, deaths, weddings, or adjustments to your real estate holdings.

In conclusion, estate planning for the purpose of real estate wealth preservation is a complex process that calls for careful thought and expert advice. Investors can ensure that their real estate investments continue to benefit future generations while minimizing potential financial responsibilities and hassles by addressing estate planning, tax efficiency, asset protection, and succession planning.

Chapter 10: Case Studies and Success Stories

Case studies and real estate investment success stories offer useful insights into the tactics that have helped investors achieve big returns and financial success. These narratives highlight the possibility of financial success and progress while illustrating various real estate investing strategies:

Case Study 1: Buy and Hold for Long-Term Growth

In this instance, a real estate investor bought a multi-family house in a developing city. The investor's plan was to purchase the asset and keep it for future expansion. The value of the property increased consistently over time, and rental income generated a steady flow of cash. Profits were invested back into the property by the investor, raising its value even more. The eventual sale of the home at a healthy profit serves as evidence of how well a patient buy-and-hold strategy may profit from the expansion of the real estate market.

Case Study 2: Fixing and Flipping for Quick Profits

A single-family home in need of repair was discovered by a real estate investor who specializes in fix-and-flip homes. The investor got the house for a good deal, fixed it up, and then sold it for a tidy profit. This example demonstrates the possibility of quick profits from well-timed property sales and planned improvements, provided the investor has a thorough understanding of market dynamics and property value.

Case Study 3: Multifamily Syndication

An experienced sponsor organized a group of investors who pooled their funds to take part in a multifamily syndication venture. Investors had access to larger, income-producing properties through syndication that they might not have otherwise had access to. The syndicated structure demonstrated the advantages of cooperation and specialized knowledge in real estate investment by providing passive income and prospective appreciation.

Case Study 4: A 1031 Exchange to Reduce Taxes

A landlord who had several rental properties sought to use a 1031 exchange to postpone paying capital gains taxes. The investor protected their wealth and increased their real estate portfolio by selling many properties and reinvesting the money into like-kind properties within the exchange deadline. This example shows how employing tax-effective measures can help maintain wealth over the long term.

Case Study 5: Development of Commercial Real Estate

An opportunity to purchase land in a developing commercial zone was spotted by a real estate developer. The developer built a commercial building with retail and office space after securing the required licenses and clearances. High-quality tenants were drawn to the development, which led to consistent rental income and property growth. This instance demonstrates the potential benefits of commercial real estate development when done in a thoughtful and calculated manner.

These case studies and success tales highlight the variety of tactics and methods that might result in real estate investment success. Additionally, they stress the significance of thorough planning, market research, risk assessment, and expert coaching in obtaining positive results. These real-world examples can serve as a source of inspiration and teach real estate investors valuable lessons for their own financial paths and goals.

10.1: Real-Life Investment Journeys

Real-world real estate investment journeys frequently include a mix of methods, difficulties, and accomplishments. These tales demonstrate the various routes individuals take to fulfill their financial ambitions and build wealth:

A. The patient accumulator is an investor.

Investor A started out in real estate with just one rental home. By carefully conserving and reinvesting rental revenue, they gradually amassed more properties throughout the years. They were able to steadily increase their portfolio because of their cautious and patient strategy. Prioritizing cash flow and real estate appreciation, they concentrated on long-term wealth growth. With each acquisition, their passive income grew, giving them more flexibility and security over their money. The experience of Investor A shows the value of consistency and patience in real estate investing.

B: The seasoned renovator

Investor B was an expert at flipping houses. They were experts at spotting undervalued houses that needed work. Investor B achieved substantial returns in a short amount of time by buying distressed houses, making cost-effective renovations, and selling them at a profit. Their success was greatly influenced by their knowledge of market trends, renovations, and property evaluation. This trip serves as an example of how market timing and strategic remodeling can result in profitable opportunities.

C. The multifamily syndicator is an investor.

Investor C was aware of the benefits of

syndication and cooperation. To take part in multifamily syndication projects, they developed relationships with other investors and an experienced sponsor. With shared duties and liabilities, this strategy gave Investor C access to larger, more profitable assets. Syndication made use of the sponsor's knowledge to provide passive income and the possibility of appreciation. The experience of Investor C demonstrates the advantages of sharing resources and expertise when making real estate investments.

D. The commercial developer is an investor.

Investor D entered the field of commercial real estate development after spotting a chance in a developing business area. They managed the difficulties of getting approvals, finding funding, and managing the building process. A variety of commercial and retail spaces were included in the development, drawing respected tenants. This calculated action produced consistent rental revenue and significant property appreciation. The experience of Investor D illustrates the potential benefits of commercial real estate development when carried out with careful planning and market knowledge.

E. The Tax-Efficiency Strategist

Investor E was knowledgeable about

tax-effective business practices. They upgraded their real estate holdings while deferring capital gains taxes by using a 1031 exchange. Investor E conserved wealth and increased their holdings by disposing of properties and reinvesting the earnings into properties of a similar type within the exchange timetable. The significance of tax-efficient preparation in real estate investment is brought home by this voyage.

These actual investing trips show that there are different paths to real estate success. Investors can achieve their financial goals by matching their approach with their goals, utilizing their strengths, and navigating the particular challenges of the real estate market, whether through patient accumulation, renovation expertise, syndication, development, or tax-efficiency strategies. Each journey serves as a reminder of how crucial flexibility and a thoughtful strategy are while pursuing real estate investment success.

10.2: Advice from savvy investors

For those wishing to start their own investment journeys, successful real estate investors may frequently be great sources of knowledge and motivation. Insights and lessons from their experiences can help aspiring investors achieve financial success.

1. Diversification and Risk Management: Diversification is a key concept for many successful investors. Investors can lower their risk and lessen the effects of economic volatility by distributing their investments over a variety of property types, regions, and markets. Building a diversified real estate portfolio is an important approach.

2. Long-Term Perspective: Successful investors frequently exhibit patience and a long-term outlook. They are aware that investing in real estate is a long-term strategy for wealth accumulation rather than a quick way to get rich. Investors can profit from property appreciation while navigating market ups and downs by concentrating on the long-term potential of assets.

3. Market Research and Due Diligence: For successful investors, thorough market research and due diligence are essential. They take the time to comprehend the state of the local economy, the worth of properties, and the rental market. Their investing choices are informed by this information, which also aids them in spotting possibilities that support their objectives.

4. Ongoing Learning: Investors who succeed are lifelong learners. They keep up with market developments, legislative changes, and real estate industry changes. They gain the knowledge and agility necessary to make wise decisions in a changing industry thanks to ongoing education.

5. Professional Partnerships: A lot of investors stress the value of assembling a team of experts, such as real estate brokers, lawyers, financial consultants, and property managers. Through these collaborations, the investment process is supported and given access to invaluable experience.

6. Financial savvy: Successful investors frequently possess financial literacy. They are aware of the financial ramifications of real estate, such as tax issues, financing choices, and cash flow analysis. They are able to make risk- and return-adjusted financial decisions because of this knowledge.

7. Flexibility: Since real estate markets can be erratic, investors must be flexible to shifting conditions. Successful investors are adaptable and willing to change their plans in response to changes in the market and the overall state of the economy.

8. Resilience: The real estate path is not without difficulties and setbacks. In the face of difficulty, resilient investors show strength. They keep trying, keep their resolve, and persevere in order to achieve their financial objectives.

9. Goal-setting: Successful investors always have clear, attainable goals for their investments. Goals give direction and incentive, assisting investors in making decisions about their investments and maintaining focus on their goals.

10. Ethical Practices: Long-term success in real

estate investing depends on upholding honest and ethical standards in all facets of the business. Being ethical builds trust with customers, business partners, and the community, which ultimately helps build a solid reputation and long-term success.

Studying their tactics, adopting best practices, and applying these lessons to one's own investment path are all part of learning from successful investors. The values of diversity, diligence, ongoing learning, and ethical behavior serve as a strong basis for real estate investment success, even though each investor's journey may be different.

Chapter 11: Buy-and-Hold Real Estate in the Future

In the constantly changing real estate market, the buy and hold real estate investment strategy, which entails purchasing properties for long-term ownership, is still a feasible and promising strategy. For buy-and-hold investors, a number of trends and characteristics indicate a promising future:

1. Growing Population and Urbanization: Urbanization tendencies continue as the world's population expands. The demand for rental homes in metropolitan regions is rising as more people relocate to cities. Owners of properties in prime locations who are buy-and-hold investors can profit from this change in the population.

2. Rental Market Stability: Historically, buy-and-hold investors have greatly benefited from the rental market's stability. Despite possible fluctuations in property values, rental income often generates a steady cash flow, providing both financial security and passive income streams.

3. Long-Term Appreciation: Long-term property appreciation is often given priority by buy-and-hold investors. Property values tend to increase over time, enabling investors to accumulate equity and potentially make sizable gains when selling in the future.

4. Tax Benefits: Buy-and-hold investments are tax-efficient due to tax advantages like depreciation deductions and the option to postpone paying capital gains taxes through 1031 exchanges. Overall returns and asset preservation may be improved by these advantages.

5. Rental Technology: For buy-and-hold investors, technological advancements have revolutionized property management. Operations have been streamlined by property management software, online listing services, and smart home technology, which makes it simpler to find and keep renters while maximizing the performance of properties.

6. Sustainability and green investing: Both tenants and investors are placing increased value on sustainable practices and energy-efficient real estate. Investors that promote eco-friendly amenities may draw eco-aware tenants while also reaping the rewards of energy savings and potential incentives.

7. Low Interest Rates: For buy-and-hold investors, borrowing may be more inexpensive thanks to favorable interest rates. Low borrowing costs can facilitate the purchase of new properties and increase cash-on-cash returns.

8. Multifamily and Mixed-Use Properties: Buy-and-hold investors are increasingly

149

attracted to multifamily and mixed-use properties. Financial stability is increased by the diversification and opportunity for many revenue streams provided by these property types.

9. Demographic Changes: The demand for various types of rental properties, such as senior housing and micro-apartments, is being driven by the aging population and changing lifestyles. Buy-and-hold investors can benefit from changing tenant preferences if they adjust to these demographic shifts.

10. Flexibility and Adaptability: Buy-and-hold investors are able to adjust to shifting economic cycles and market conditions. This strategy offers flexibility to align with financial objectives, whether holding through market swings or changing rental plans.

In summary, continuous demographic trends, rental market stability, tax advantages, technological developments, and sustainable business practices all point to a bright future for buy-and-hold real estate. The purchase and hold approach to real estate investing will continue to be profitable for investors that follow these patterns, keep a long-term view, and keep up with market developments.

11.1: Trends to Watch

Economic, social, and technical forces continuously reshape the real estate investing landscape. Investors should be aware of new trends that may affect their prospects and strategies.

Integration of technology: The real estate sector is changing as a result of technology. Investors should keep an eye out for innovations that improve property management and tenant experiences, such as blockchain for real estate transactions, artificial intelligence for data-driven decisions, and smart home technology.

Sustainability and ESG: Environmental, Social, and Governance (ESG) factors are becoming more and more important in the real estate industry. It is important to keep an eye on trends that affect tenant preferences and market demand, such as investments in sustainable and green projects and adherence to morally and socially responsible behavior.

Impact of Remote Work: The demand for office space is changing as a result of the increase in remote work. Investors should be aware of how trends in remote work may affect the commercial real estate market, including potential changes in demand for coworking spaces and flexible office solutions.

Multifamily Housing: Demand for multifamily housing is being impacted by demographic changes, such as an aging population and shifting household composition. Investors want to keep an eye out for openings in the senior housing, micro-apartment, and other market segments that are in line with changing tenant needs.

Proptech and Innovation: New tools for investment analysis, tenant interaction, and property management are always being developed in the proptech industry. Investors want to look into proptech advances that can improve productivity and judgment.

Affordable housing initiatives give investors

chances as a result of the affordability crisis that is affecting many places. Tax incentives and public-private collaborations might help address this issue.

The hospitality and rental industries have been affected by short-term rental platforms like Airbnb. To determine if short-term rental investments are viable, investors should keep an eye on regulatory changes and regional market trends.

The COVID-19 epidemic has accelerated migratory patterns into rural and suburban areas, which is item #8. As preferences change, investors should assess the possibilities for rental and investment options in these areas.

Remote Investing: It's getting easier to invest in real estate remotely. Investors want to think about how remote platforms and prospects for investing in real estate can increase their real estate holdings.

Economic indicators, such as interest rates, inflation, and economic expansion, have an impact on real estate investment. It is crucial to keep up with economic indicators and their potential impact on real estate prices and financing costs.

Regulatory Modifications: Investment plans can be significantly impacted by real estate legislation. Investors should stay informed of changes to local and federal regulations, including zoning rules, rent control legislation, and tax restrictions.

The COVID-19 epidemic has raised awareness of health and wellbeing in real estate. Investors want to take into account buildings and amenities that put tenants' health first, like ventilation systems and outdoor areas.

In order to make wise judgments and adjust to a changing market, real estate investors must constantly be aware of these patterns and any potential ramifications. Adaptable investors make use of new trends to seize opportunities and successfully deal with obstacles.

11.2: Making Plans for Upcoming Opportunities

For real estate investors hoping to take advantage of future opportunities in a constantly shifting market, proactive planning is essential. Here are some strategies to consider:

1. Education and Knowledge: Continue to deepen your understanding of local market dynamics, investment tactics, and real estate trends. To network and get knowledge from other investors, go to seminars, webinars, and industry events. You might also want to join real estate investment associations.

2. Market research: Keep up with developments in the markets you are targeting. Analyze property valuations, rental patterns, and economic factors on a regular basis. You can spot investment possibilities by comprehending market cycles and spotting growing neighborhoods.

3. Financial Readiness: Establish and keep up a strong credit history, keep an eye on your debt-to-income ratio, and put money aside for future investments. Being prepared financially enables you to seize opportunities when they present themselves.

4. Diversification: To spread risk, think about

diversifying your real estate holdings. To lessen exposure to local market changes, investigate several property kinds, such as residential, commercial, and multifamily, or diversify regionally.

5. Establishing a Network: Develop connections with real estate experts, such as agents, brokers, property managers, and contractors. A strong network can give access to off-market deals, important insights, and reliable partners for joint ventures.

6. Optimize your property management procedures to increase efficiency: Investigate the software and technologies for property management that can increase tenant communication, streamline processes, and boost overall effectiveness.

7. Technology Adoption: Use technology to your advantage to stay competitive. To reach potential tenants or buyers and make data-driven decisions, investigate real estate investing software, data analytics tools, and digital marketing methods.

8. Tax Planning: Collaborate with tax experts to create tax-effective plans. Your ability to maximize returns and protect your capital depends on your understanding of tax incentives, deductions, and 1031 exchanges.

9. Risk assessment: constantly evaluate and

control risks. Perform complete due diligence on potential investments, including market research, tenant screening, and property inspections. Be ready for any unforeseen difficulties that can occur when making an investment.

10. Flexibility: Be adaptable and flexible in your approach to investing. Market conditions can change quickly, so be prepared to modify your plan in response to new possibilities or changes in the economy.

11. Long-Term Vision: Keep an eye on the big picture when making investments. Real estate frequently rewards patient investors who concentrate on creating wealth over the long term, despite the allure of short-term gains.

12. Market Monitoring: Keep an eye out for changes in regulations, economic news, and market movements. Be ready to adjust your investment approach if necessary to reflect changing market conditions.

Real estate investors can position themselves to take advantage of good offers, adjust to shifting market conditions, and meet their financial objectives by anticipating and proactively addressing upcoming possibilities and problems. An informed and well-prepared investor is better able to successfully negotiate the complexity of real estate investment.

Chapter 12: Conclusion and Action Plan

Success in the fast-paced world of real estate investing depends on both where you are now and how effectively you plan for the future. To sum up the main ideas mentioned, The key concepts are as follows, in brief:

Real estate investment trends: Keep up with the latest developments in areas including remote working, sustainability, and affordable housing. The real estate market will change as a result of these movements, opening up new possibilities.

Education and understanding: Make a commitment to continual learning and market research to increase your real estate understanding. Participate in industry gatherings, join organizations, and monitor market trends.

Financial Readiness: Keep your finances in good shape by managing your credit, keeping an eye on your finances, and setting aside money for future investments. You can respond quickly to opportunities when you are financially prepared.

Consider diversifying your portfolio to lower risk by looking at various property types and geographic areas.

Building a network means establishing and maintaining connections with real estate experts who might present beneficial possibilities and insights.

Efficient Property Management: To increase productivity and tenant satisfaction, optimize property management procedures using tools and technology.

Technology Adoption: Use technology to make data-driven decisions and to effectively target prospective tenants or buyers through digital marketing methods.

Planning for taxes: Develop tax-effective

solutions with the help of tax experts to increase returns and protect capital.

Assessing and managing risks connected with possible investments requires careful due diligence. Be ready for unforeseen difficulties.

Adaptability: Be flexible and adaptable in your investment strategy and be prepared to change course when the market environment requires it.

Maintain a long-term perspective since patient investors who concentrate on accumulating money over time are frequently awarded in real estate.

Market Watching: Be on the lookout for

changes in regulations, economic news, and market movements so you can make any required adjustments to your investing strategy.

Now is the time to apply what you have learned. Make an action plan that is specific and specifies the activities you will take to become ready for potential real estate investing opportunities.

Set Specific Investment Objectives: Establish your financial goals, whether they are generating passive income, long-term wealth, or a combination of the two.

Market Research: Based on in-depth market research, choose target markets, taking development potential, rental demand, and economic stability into account.

Networking: Create and grow your contact list of real estate brokers, builders, and property managers.

Planning your finances: Determine your level of financial preparedness and make the necessary changes to improve your financial condition.

Property management: Use technology and effective management techniques to streamline your property management procedures.

Technology Integration: To improve your

investment operations, research and apply pertinent real estate technology tools.

Tax Planning: Speak with tax experts to create a tax-efficient plan that is specific to your investing objectives.

Risk management: Establish due diligence procedures and protocols for assessing the risks of potential investments.

Develop backup plans and coping mechanisms for adjusting to shifting market circumstances.

Education: Make a commitment to lifelong learning by going to conferences, webinars, and trade shows.

Maintain a patient, long-term investment approach that is in line with your financial objectives.

Regular Review: Make sure your action plan is consistently reviewed and updated to be in line with your changing investment strategy.

You'll be ready to take advantage of new possibilities, adjust to market changes, and accomplish your real estate investment goals if you stick to your action plan. Keep in mind that making money in real estate involves commitment, flexibility, and a desire for lifelong learning and development.